Many Miles

Cover art: Rosa Sophia, personal photograph of Miles
Cover and interior design: Brianna Chapman
Editor: Jessie Truong
Publisher: Allison Blevins
Director: Kristiane Weeks-Rogers

MANY MILES
ROSA SOPHIA GODSHALL
ISBN 978-1-957248-46-2
Harbor Editions,
an imprint of Small Harbor Publishing

Many Miles

Rosa Sophia Godshall

Harbor Editions
Small Harbor Publishing

Contents

Many Miles

The woods are lovely, dark and deep,
But I have promises to keep,
And miles to go before I sleep,
And miles to go before I sleep.

—Robert Frost

Infinite Baffle

Infinite baffle
Noun: Audio.
*1. a loudspeaker enclosure that totally separates sound
emanating from the rear of the speaker cone
from sound emanating in front, so as to prevent mutual interference.*

we were only children   when she taught us death is a choice

      my mother gave twisted permissions   like a damaged
audio system   and because her wires were bare and corroded
she had no awareness

crank the volume   hear the interference

      suicide exists within an infinite baffle
where the sound of the gunshot never stops
the sound trapped   inside this loudspeaker baffle   never finds passage

from infinite space

      a fuse will blow   a wire will melt   so find a certified
technician—
someone to address this weakness, my system's primary resistance

      but for now   let's lower the gain and listen—

      whenever the sun goes down   my mother shrieks
            where is my son?
I don't tell her   he never left   his hands are on my shoulders

his spirit is at my back

PHILADELPHIA POLICE DEPARTMENT INCIDENT REPORT

CRIME OR INCIDENT
CLASSIFICATION
Suicide

DATE OF OCCUR
8-22-15

NATURE OF INJURY
Gunshot / head

DESCRIPTION OF INCIDENT
Pronounced by medic at 11:40PM.
Suspicious death.Medical examiner
notified.

MEDICAL EXAMINER

How did you know the deceased?

He is still my brother.

My Machine

I flip the switch, turn on the air compressor,
hook up the half-inch impact gun, press
the trigger, watch the silver socket whirl.

This engine listens to me, speaks to me
in numbers and equations: force exerted in its cylinders,
the diameter of its bore, calculated easier

than I can calculate myself, the dyscalculia
in my brain twisting numbers into other digits.
I stare at its washers, mounts, torque-to-yield

head bolts, camshaft, crankshaft, cylinder head,
sleepy gaskets nestled inside, easily damaged,
I tear it down as I tear away my flesh,

scraping weak gaskets from smooth metal exteriors,
breathing deep into the carburetor, exhaling life
into cavities and radiator hoses,

my bones becoming the tool I use to hone
these cylinders. My arms, like pistons, dive deep
inside. I am the bolts and washers, the mounts and brackets.

I have become my machine.

Miles

When I met you, I was 33. This means you'll never know my little brother Miles because he shot himself when I was 29 and he was 27. You'll never know Miles and I laugh the same way, blow our noses the same way, even apply Old Spice deodorant the same way. We wore the same size shoes, same size shirts and jeans. I can tell you these things, but you'll never meet him, never sit with him and listen to his discourses on Wing Chun, Shim Gum Do, and why he felt Alexander the Great was "a ruthless murdering cross-dresser with a propensity for young boys."

You'll never see him practicing the first set of Wing Chun forms in my kitchen. You'll never know how protective he was of anyone who needed defending. You'll never have first-hand knowledge of the calls I made after I talked to the medical examiner—how I dissociated so I could drive to my mother's house in Juno Beach, knock on the door and say, *Mama, your little boy killed himself.*

You'll never be linked to me that way. You'll never know the sharp intake of breath I heard on the other line when I said to my uncle, *your nephew killed himself.* How I remember so clearly the exact space in which I stood in my mother's driveway when I called my cousin and said, *Miles killed himself,* exactly a year after my cousin's boy did the same. You'll never know how I feared telling our grandparents in Pennsylvania, so I asked other people to do it, to have them sit down, make sure they were comfortable, safe, to listen to these words—*your grandson shot himself.*

You'll never know the way my body thrummed when I dialed Miles's fiancée—I was standing by the back door in my old house, my cottage by the sea, staring out the window—and I said, *you need to sit down, is someone with you? You aren't alone, are you?*

You'll never know how much I wanted to hold her in my arms when I said, *April, Miles is gone.* The sound of her sobs as she slumped to the ground are embedded in my skin, under it, in my cell memory like tiny pins, like the sharp needles of nerve pain that crawl across my face and scalp.

You'll never know unless I tell you that several years later, I sat with April and watched her open a bag she'd vacuum-packed with his clothes, hoping they'd still smell like him, and when they didn't, she wept, and it was then I held her.

You'll never know unless I tell you that Miles and I were given permission to believe in suicide, to believe in its validity as an option, with the same casualness of choosing between pumpkin pie and apple pie at the grocery store—by the way, you'd never know this, but pumpkin pie was Miles's favorite and he ate it from his hands, never used a napkin. One time in high school when he was high, he hid warm brownies in his pockets, then ate them, lint and all.

You'll never know unless I tell you that I am like my grandmother, her mother, and her mother before her because I can see the unseen, reach the in-between. I see what lies beyond because in my visions I journey and converse with the dead. And I am telling you: We were children who took care of a mother who drank too much and talked about suicide, suicide, suicide.

You'll never know unless I tell you that Miles went blind once when we were kids after drinking too much moonshine he found in the cellar, and we wondered how long it had been there, and my mother said, *maybe it belonged to Hans*, her friend who lived there in the 1970s and died of cancer. You'll never know the terror I felt watching him scream, cry, run into walls, shouting, *I can't see, I can't see, I can't see*. Looking back, I wonder if we shared the same affliction, ocular migraines crawling from the brain, obscuring our vision.

You'll never know Miles found a way to keep his feet warm in the winter by lighting the bottoms of his socks on fire and watching the flame jump to his toes. You'll never know he blew his nose on those same socks, didn't see a need for tissues, made a habit of pissing out his bedroom window.

You'll never know unless I tell you, I tailgate eighteen-wheelers because Miles always said it improves your gas mileage, and when you're close, real close, you can feel the pulsing wind of the beast before you. He said, *that's the sweet spot, don't leave it. Let it take you where you need to go.* You'll never know unless I tell you, he was my twin even though he wasn't. He carried our mother's pain. How much of his pain do I carry?

Like a Rider in a Chariot

After the Katha Upanishad

In neutral I press the clutch, turn the key. The engine opens its mouth and speaks to me. I must switch on the headlights if I wish to see. Some don't: Heading north from Miami in the middle of the night, a dark shape weaves in and out of traffic with nothing to light its way. The body is the chariot. I consider how I turn, steering column and drivetrain under my direction. Many miles later I take the Juno Beach exit and drive to the ocean. I park and walk under the palms. I once said I left my soul here, wrote *this is my home* in the sand. Which part of you hears me when I'm speaking, your soul or your machine? Listen to the purr of the pistons.

we want to transform
but no manual can help—
we sit in our seat, seek silence

Infinite Baffle

he is still my brother:

      years ago I met him in a parking lot when his car wouldn't start
hooked my cables to his terminals

explained negative, positive   listened to the hum of my engine

sending energy to him

      sometimes in car audio we cut power   think our system
needs fresh speakers

when the answer was always an amplifier   filtering noise

from infinite space

      my brother knew I was a mechanic, took my training at Lincoln
Tech, but sometimes there are machines   I can never fix

      when the medical examiner called, I said
I wish I'd seen my brother's distance   *wish I'd lowered the gain to listen*
      but I know, I know—

      I have my own ways of turning inward   slicing wires
ripping out my harnesses   shutting down my crackling sound system

in order to find the silence

FINDINGS

Gunshot wound to the head

     a. Entrance: right temple; soot present on the surrounding skin

     b. Injury to the bilateral temporal bones

     c. Projectile recovered from the soft tissue of the left temporal area

     d. Direction: from right to left without significant anteroposterior or vertical deviation

Cause of Death: Gunshot Wound to the Head
Manner of Death: Suicide

MEDICAL EXAMINER   Were there any signs?

I never knew he wanted to die.

Diode

A diode provides a one-way path for current. A good example is a headlight switch: The switch turns on, or off. The current flows, or it doesn't. Think about that when you switch on your headlights, watch the bright beam illuminate the garage door in front of you. It only takes one direction.

But I am a Zener diode: When a certain voltage is reached, I change directions. I can't tell you when or if or how. My voltage is fluid.

Our circuits have been connected. I don't care what physical form you've taken.

You can understand that—can't you?

Miles

I remember you—my little brother—rolling tobacco from the butts of other people's cigarettes. Mama taught us not to waste. When I'm out to dinner with friends, if someone doesn't finish, I'll ask, *are you going to eat that?*

I'm sure you remember how I pride myself on being somebody who will eat whatever others leave behind. When I lived in the trailer park on the Treasure Coast, I picked up all the bruised mangos that fell from the tree. No one else wanted them. It was six years ago, when you were still alive, and I've moved 70 miles north, but I still have some in my freezer because I don't want to know what it's like to be without them.

When people die, they leave food behind. I still have your jar of dried kidney beans in the kitchen. The jar was among your belongings after they found your body in Philadelphia. A friend packed everything in the trunk of your car, which trapped the scent of your corpse. She warned me about this because no one knew how long you'd been lying in your apartment before the police found you. I remember the smell. This is what I think of when I see your jar of kidney beans.

I remember the rice, but I don't remember whether it was in a jar. We held the memorial at our old high school and someone decided to cook the rice from your apartment. They couldn't cook all of it. One container had weevils. It felt like eating a part of you.

I remember how you listened, how you nodded while sharpening a switchblade on a whetstone, a cigarette hanging from the corner of your mouth. You were always hurting yourself.

Remember that time you were drunk and high and you sliced your hand open on a ninja star? Mama screamed, but she wouldn't let anyone call an ambulance because the house was full of underage kids drinking booze. At some point you recovered, your hand wrapped in a duct-taped t-shirt. Remember how you always said, *if you can't 'duck' it, fuck it?* We found you eating a large pizza on the floor of the bathroom.

I remember the beginning, which feels like the end. When I was six and you were four, Mama made us run away from home. The three of us hid behind a shed in the woods, our backs to the corrugated metal wall.

Fifteen years later, I decided to find our father's side of the family, even though Mama didn't like me doing this. Do you remember? She told us Grandmom and Grandpop didn't really love us, but that Thanksgiving, they welcomed us into their home—we were strangers—and we ate mashed potatoes, corn, steamed broccoli, pie and Jell-O desserts and Grandmom's famous cherry-cheese.

It was too late. I remember how we got to know our father, and then he was crushed by a four-wheeler. They kept him alive for a year as a vegetable.

When I tell the stories, I laugh because I have to. I tell people I fabricated everything from a *Days of Our Lives* episode, but that isn't true. I've never even seen the show, so maybe I'm off-base and nothing like our lives could've happened on a sound stage.

I remember how you sat still against the wall of the shed in the woods that day when you were four, your eyes dry, your hair still blond, then. As you grew, it would darken, turn tree-trunk brown.

When you were 27, Dad was already dead, and you were always changing your number so Mama couldn't find you. You had the same look on your face two months before you shot yourself. I remember how your eyes said, *nothing has changed in 23 years.*

I remember when you helped me move. You made a cheese sandwich for me. You never used dishes. You liked spicy mustard. You took your own sandwich outside and sat on the stoop to eat. I said, *thank you, Miles,* and I joined you, and we ate, together.

Quit Claim

Quitclaim:
a legal instrument used to release one person's right, title, or interest to another
without providing a guarantee or warranty of title

Quit claim deed.
Property Appraiser's Parcel Identification No. 28-36-27-KN-1783-2.
This Quit Claim Deed, Executed this 19th day of August, 2020.

Today I file a quitclaim deed for the empty lot beside my house:
The house once belonged to my cousin Gregg, where he used to recline
on his sofa, drink rum and Coke and laugh and remember
his youth before he got sick.

Given by (first party) my cousin Gregg,
my brother Miles who shot himself on this day in 2015,
my great-grandmother, born on this day in 1900,
who helped raise Gregg after his mother's murder

all those who've gone before me, whose corporeal forms
transitioned into ashes, whose eyes gazed into the sharp corner
where the ceiling meets the wall, just before they exhaled,
inhaled, exhaled for the very last time.

On my bookshelves I keep human ashes, locks of hair,
Gram's braid, gray and silver, wound tight, other people's treasures.
One day I will die, which means all these items don't really matter:
Where will they go when I no longer have hands to hold them?

To (second party) myself,
living now in a single-family home in Palm Bay, Florida—
Gregg's former home—with peeling paint
and my dead father's Jeep sitting in a dusty one-car garage.

All ownership is transitory, prepared by the cosmos.

Witnesseth:

*The said first party has paid the said second party for the lot of empty land
beside this house. The first party does hereby release and quit claim unto
the second party forever—all the right, claim and demand to the parcel.*

*

Witnesseth:

I remember when my cousin told me he was dying,
he asked, "Would you like to live in my house?" I said yes, sure,
because I thought five years, ten—not one. Only one year?

But I remember the day his eyes turned yellow, his eyes changed color,
and I remember four years ago we walked into this courthouse
and my cousin, his almost-four-hundred-pounds
leaning on a wooden cane,
tried to file a quit claim deed, and the clerk said,
"You know it'll be hers now, right?"

Witnesseth:

Instead of filing it with him, I filed it the day after he died:
He'd already prepared his signature on the bottom line,
giving me everything
in his last will and testament, telling me months before he left,
"You're more of a daughter to me than a cousin."

The day before he died, I looked into his eyes and saw the toddler
who watched his mother's murder from his playpen,
his father's hunting knife piercing her chest,
and I couldn't help but wonder,
did that memory repeat every day of his life?

Today as I file the quit claim deed for the lot beside the house,
the clerk at the window drinks from a mug
exactly like the set Gregg owned:
The mug isn't all that remarkable,
a green and tan abstract design on white.
The clerk sets down her mug, beckons to me, the next person in line.

I turn around, part of me expecting to see my cousin, but of course,
he's not there. The last of his ashes held in a cardboard box, tucked away
in a dresser drawer of what used to his bedroom—my bedroom now.

I sleep in his bed. I sit in his favorite chair. I take care of his cat.
I wander the small house, alone, looking, talking to him as if he's there.
I keep his faux leather loafers where he left them, toes facing
the television, as if waiting for his feet to return.

*In witness whereof, the first party has signed and sealed, the day and year first above
written.*

Signed and sealed and delivered in the presence of the cosmos.
Prepared by _____.

Sparring Methods

To be forced to fight the self is a terrible pity.
—Miles

At a Wing Chun school with men three times my size
I practice sparring methods. My brother is dead:

He wrote a book on martial arts
and I'm trying to understand him.

My sifu is a roofer who teaches self-defense
on days and nights off. He lifts his hands

in front of his chest and tells us it's time
to learn sparring methods.

My brother always taught me to protect
my centerline against attack.

My sifu the roofer pairs off the class
to teach us the one-handed sparring method.

We each place one hand behind our backs,
one hand in front, fingers pointing up.

I think of my brother practicing forms,
teaching his students sparring methods.

In the years before his suicide, my brother
sent an email with the heading Public Service:

He listed terms of combat, his self-designed techniques
and recommended sparring methods.

My brother is dead: he once wrote,
Reach out, see that? You're touching the limits

of your sphere of influence. He learned Chi Sao,
advancing his knowledge of sparring methods.

20

I realize my deadliest opponent was always myself.
If my brother's like me, maybe he believed he'd win

if he knew every form, every movement,
every single sparring method.

My sifu tells us we'll practice with a blindfold.
My partner is a lean, muscular pro-MMA fighter

who's visiting our class for the day,
here to teach us sparring methods.

This man has lost and won fights, seen bets
placed in his favor, and now he's lifting his hands

against his partner, a woman who feels like a scared girl
about to learn sparring methods. My brother is dead:

I wish he could see his sister squaring off
with a fighter who says, *I can tell you're nervous.*

Don't worry, you can do this,
while learning sparring methods.

In the years before my brother's suicide, my centerline
was a wide-open door. I shut the door when he pulled the trigger,

lifted my arms to study sparring methods.
Another term for Chi Sao is sticky hands:

My hands make contact with my opponent,
with every move their hands stick to mine—

an eternal loop of energy within a sparring method.
I wish I'd learned from my brother when he was alive,

looked into his eyes—been a better sister,
let my brother teach me sparring methods.

Impact / Gun

My Earthquake-brand impact gun connected to my air compressor
removes the axle bolt in seconds / but there's still the job of slamming
the hub to release the captive rotor

As a teenager I learned to disconnect battery cables / minimize amperage
cut power / replace tapping valves with silence

As a teenager locks meant nothing / my brother Miles slammed
his drunken body against my bedroom door causing wood to crack /
the frame to slide against the wall

As a teenager Miles rolled cigarettes with Mama / together they hung
a map on the wall and imagined all the places they'd go

As a teenager Miles listened to Mama / I played interference / like a box
wrench held on the back of a bolt to make the socket do its work /
I kept her from hurting herself

All these years later my impact gun has a comfortable weight / makes me
feel like I can do anything / without it I crank on a breaker bar /
how will I ever finish this job?

My Earthquake-brand impact gun connected to my air compressor gives
me the strength I've missed / while Miles found release with a Bersa .380
semi-automatic pistol / the ease of pulling the trigger against the smooth
skin of his head

The impact of his leftovers / a martial arts dummy ready for sparring /
a fencing sword, a wooden staff / his voice on the edge of my hearing

I connect an air hose to my impact gun and pull the trigger / sometimes
it feels like a tool can solve everything / but when I pull the hub from
the rotor the bearings fall out in my hand

Drag Track Haibun

After Palm Beach International Raceway

The air's thick with high-test fuel in mid-July as a dragster revs on the straightaway shooting flames. Cars line up to wait their turn on test-and-tune night, experimental races, so some of the cars are funky beat-up relics like a Subaru with broken weather-stripping and peeling paint. A Chevy snaps a rod on the straightaway, an engine dies at the finish line. Eleven years pass. Some nights I pop awake and feel afraid. If only I could go back and run my hands across a Barracuda's hood, I'd gain some comfort encased in rust and chrome. At first we begged for speed; now we're yearning for the putt-putt of a four-banger grocery-getter. Remember how we watched the seconds at the track, cheered when time was beaten?

How many moments?
I need an engine to tend—
body quick to fix

Miles

These are things I don't say often: Human ashes are heavier than they look, but not as heavy as the intake manifold on my pickup truck. Inherited talent made me into a good mechanic, post-traumatic stress made me into a better one. Engines are like people, they're just easier to fix.

The paperwork of death becomes so much harder when it's suicide. Every person I talk to says, *are you the executor of the estate?* And I say, *no, my little brother shot himself, there wasn't time for that,* and there's silence as if we're expected to know, prepare ahead like morbid fortune tellers. Hearse-chasers are a thing even if there's no hearse, just paperwork, just me, just a woman drinking tea in an empty living room.

This is something I never tell anyone: a thread of twisted sexual tension thrummed through my childhood like a bad dream. My humiliation is fierce. Sometimes my relationship with my little brother felt incestuous. We didn't know how to love each other the right way, so we focused on surviving.

You'll never know unless I tell you: pot seeds littered our kitchen. Half-smoked joints rested in ashtrays. The cupboards were never clean. Mice toddled across puke-yellow broken counters, unafraid in daylight, seeking crumbs, running across the top of the bookshelf in the corner.

When I dream about this house, it's always night, everything is broken, and someone's always out to hurt me. I wondered if the mice would eat my books. Sometimes I checked the pages looking for bite marks. One day in high school, Miles and his friend were in the kitchen smoking, drinking. As I walked by the table, Miles grabbed my ass and said, *if you weren't my sister—*

I wasn't safe, but Miles wasn't either. In elementary school, his guidance counselor molested him. We didn't find out until after he pulled the trigger. He only mentioned it while drunk, like so many other things he never talked about while sober.

You'll never know unless I tell you: Miles was an angry drunk. He threw his body against my bedroom door so many times the frame disconnected from the wall. If I could go back, I would open the door. Let him hit me if he needed to. Then hold him. Hold him while he cried. Because years later, I learned we were exactly the same. Both of us just needed to cry.

This is something I never told anyone: I decided not to have children because I feared I might abuse them. My mother passed down to me her deepest terrors, and they wound into my nightmares like the roots of the Virginia creeper vine that grew along the stucco walls of our dumpy house, so deep and hard to pull.

My mother and I had the same fear as children—that we would come home one day and find the house burned to the ground. Because my mother talked about sex and promiscuity and abuse when I was a child, I thought sex the only way to demonstrate affection. The disembodied voices I used to hear, which sometimes emerged from objects that wobbled, seemed to suggest I might love someone the wrong way because it's the only way I know.

The voices reminded me of my worthlessness, sexualized every kind of affection or tinged it with violence. I covered my ears, but I could still hear them. Sometimes I still do. I feel uncomfortable whenever a hug seems to last too long, because no one ever told me about normal love—just the abnormal kind that kills the heart and poisons the brain. So, you'll never know unless I tell you, my heart's always been broken, and I keep patching it like somebody using fix-a-flat in an old tire, a temporary solution everyone knows will never last.

You'll never know unless I tell you, I had no safe place, no privacy. At fifteen while my mother drank in the next room, my rapist—an older boy from school—took what he wanted from me. When I said, *no, please stop, please stop*, he laughed. And laughed. And laughed.

And that's why, years later, I tell April, *the better someone treats me, the more suspicious I get—because what do they want from me? What are they hoping to claim, abuse, discard? And how do I know this goodness isn't just a cheap veneer, and that once I'm comfortable, it'll fall away to reveal the rot beneath?* April tells me, *you are*

Miles's sister—he would have said the same exact thing. I am Miles's twin, even though I'm not.

These are things I don't say often: when Miles shot himself, some people told me he would burn in eternal damnation. But what kind of God would condemn a suffering child? Because that's what we both were, suffering, our childhood threaded with twisted sexual tension. Human ashes are heavier than they look, but not as heavy as the intake manifold on my pickup truck.

And it's for all these reasons I became a mechanic, took apart engines, nestled myself between the concrete floor and a rusted frame. I feel safe under there. If my engine breaks down, I will take it apart and put it back together. There's a gentle hum, a quiet poetry in rust and chrome, the way it sits there being nothing other than what it appears. The way it exists—just is, just being. The way it endures without any reason for ending. This is something I don't say often: *Is it even possible for someone like me to love and be loved?*

I run my fingers along the bottom of this rusted frame. Where do the fissures stop? How much of my inheritance is what I am destined to become?

The Way of the Divine

After Jean Toomer

We are machines, but we can find consciousness if we work hard enough.

When the tension between us rises, I begin to see if I don't work on myself—if I don't maintain all the components of my engine—my connection will suffer.

To understand mutual capacitance, I must first understand self-capacitance.

It is said that humans are machines and by observing ourselves, we can witness the evidence.

I splice a wire, mend a connection. I am no different than my bedraggled truck engine.

Infinite Baffle

I never knew he wanted to die. I remember walking along the graveled driveway toward our house by the creek, the white stucco visible through the trees. My brother said he knew about the girl I loved, the way we concealed our kisses behind doors and in dark corners. I felt so full of shame. I needed to know I could lean on my brother's strong shoulder. The sun dappled the rippling creek, the oak trees full of foliage in the lilting summer heat. He lit a cigarette, leaned against the Ford Taurus in the driveway. I asked him not to tell. He said, "I won't. It's okay. I promise."

I hold space for you—
your presence tightly wound in this
infinite baffle

PHILADELPHIA POLICE DEPARTMENT INCIDENT REPORT

CRIME OR INCIDENT
CLASSIFICATION
Shame

DATE OF OCCUR
Infinite

NATURE OF INJURY
Baffle

DESCRIPTION OF INCIDENT
System shutdown

MEDICAL EXAMINER

What kind of person was he?

He is still my brother.

Acknowledgements

Many thanks to the following publications in which my poems have appeared and the contests in which my work has been a finalist or semifinalist:

"Miles," page 10, Thimble Literary Magazine, Summer 2023, semifinalist in the Sandy Crimmins National Prize for Poetry, 2022; finalist in Bellingham Review's 2021 Annie Dillard Award for Creative Nonfiction.

"Infinite Baffle," Landlocked Literary Magazine, 2024; finalist in the CRAFT 2022 Hybrid Writing Contest.

Rosa Sophia Godshall's work has been published in *Philadelphia Stories Magazine, Sentience Literary Journal, SoFloPoJo, Islandia Journal, Thimble Literary Magazine, Limp Wrist*, and others. She is also the author of *Village of North Palm Beach: A History* (The History Press, 2020). She was the recipient of the 2023 Christopher F. Kelly Award for Poetry, sponsored by the Academy of American Poets, through Florida International University. She holds an MFA in Creative Writing and a degree in automotive technology. She is also the managing editor of *Mobile Electronics magazine*, a publication for the aftermarket car audio industry. Rosa lives in Palm Bay, Florida, where she enjoys working on her 1960 Jeep CJ5, repairing typewriters and writing typewriter poetry on demand. Visit her website to learn more: www.torquesgarage.com

About Small Harbor Publishing

Small Harbor Publishing is a 501c3 nonprofit organization. Our goal is to publish unique and diverse voices. We are a feminist press, and we are committed to diversity and inclusion. We strive to bring new voices to a devoted and expanding readership.

Small Harbor Publishing began in 2018 with the first issue of *Harbor Review*. The magazine is an online space where poetry and art converse. *Harbor Review* quickly grew and now publishes reviews and runs multiple micro chapbook competitions, including the Washburn Prize and the Editor's Prize.

In July 2020, Small Harbor Publishing was officially incorporated and began Harbor Editions. Harbor Editions accepts submissions through a chapbook open reading period, a hybrid chapbook open reading period, the Marginalia Series, and the Laureate Prize.

In 2023, Harbor Anthologies began with a mission to promote texts that explore social justice issues and highlight marginalized writers.

If you would like to support Small Harbor Publishing, please visit our "About" page at smallharborpublishing.com/about.